Contents

Introduction and welcome

Maggie Appleton MBE,
Chief Executive.

Welcome to the Royal Air Force Museum

Our Museum's vision is to inspire **everyone** with the RAF story – the people who shape it and its place in our lives. As one of the UK's National Museums we use our magnificent collections to share those incredible stories. Don't miss Kevin Furniss' stunning First World War flying helmet, the oldest Spitfire Mk I in existence, our Percy the Parachuting Penguin lucky mascot, the RAF's three iconic Cold War strategic V-bombers and the magnificent VC10.

Whether you're here to immerse yourself in our collection, or for a great day out with family and friends, we hope you have a fabulous time. Do come back and check out our events programme which includes opportunities to get up close and personal to our collection, film nights, sleepovers among the aircraft, and annual favourites, the Cosford Food Festival and Spitfire 10K run.

If you'd like to keep in touch, do sign up for our free newsletter at **rafmuseum.org.uk** and check out **rafstories.org** to explore some treasures and find out how to contribute your own.

Thank you for visiting and enjoy your time with us.

Maggie Appleton MBE

RAF Cosford

RAF Cosford, the site of the RAF Museum Cosford, was opened in 1938, delivering operations training to generations of technicians and ground trade recruits. Home to the RAF's only official Air Show, RAF Cosford's educational ethos and community-mindedness make it an essential element of the RAF's presence in the Midlands.

History of RAF Cosford

Originally intended as an Aircraft Storage Unit (ASU) during a period of RAF expansion, RAF Cosford's remit was extended to include a Technical Training School to fulfil personnel requirements demanded by the threat of war. No. 2 School of Technical Training (2 SoTT) opened first, in August 1938. The ASU, named No. 9 Maintenance Unit, followed in March 1939, with the task of storing, assembling, repairing and issuing to operational units a wide range of aircraft types.

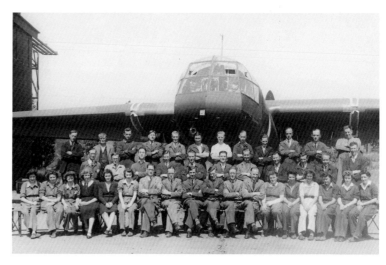

Men and women of No. 9 Maintenance Unit (MU) in front of a Horsa glider, RAF Cosford, 1945.

Princess Mary visits the RAF Hospital, Cosford, 1941.

During the Second World War, 2 SoTT trained over 70,000 airframe and engine fitters and armourers to meet the demand for ground trade technicians. Other units, including an Officer Cadet Training School, the Czechoslovak Depot, for training and dispersing Czech nationals into appropriate RAF units, a Ferry Pilots' Pool, a hospital and some prisoner-of-war reception centres were also based at Cosford. The prisoner-of war-centres received over 13,000 airmen returning from locations around Europe and the Far East, offering medical assistance and rehabilitation where needed.

Previous page: The Red Arrows at the annual Air Show at RAF Cosford.

RAF Cosford, June 1942.

Commander Marion Katherine Ogilvie Wilberforce

During the Second World War, RAF Cosford was home to 12 Ferry Pilots' Pool, an Air Transport Auxiliary (ATA) unit tasked to deliver new and repaired aircraft to operational units. From 1943 to 1945 the Pool was staffed solely by women, and Marion Wilberforce commanded the unit.

She gained her pilot's licence in 1930 and by 1945 was qualified to fly over 100 aircraft types, including Lancasters and Mosquitos. She flew privately until her 80th birthday.

> Marion Wilberforce was the quintessential 'ATA girl': resourceful, daring and skilled, with more than a touch of eccentricity in her make-up.

A chit for Spitfire Mk Vb W3656 delivered by the ATA from Scottish Aviation Limited at Prestwick to No. 9 MU Cosford for modifications on 28 September 1944.

After the Second World War the prisoner-of-war reception units were disbanded and No. 9 MU closed in 1959. Cosford Hospital was opened to civilians and remained as a community hospital until its closure in 1977.

Post-war the emphasis at RAF Cosford returned to youth training, and it became one of the principal RAF stations for Boy Entrant training. The 18-month course trained boys aged from 15 to 17 in ground trades, ranging from wireless telegraphy to catering. Three-year apprenticeships in technical subjects also became available to older boys.

Other units transferred to RAF Cosford, including the RAF School of Physical Training and the Joint School of Photography (now known as the Defence School of Photography). The training in these two subjects is now synonymous with the base.

No. 1 School of Technical Training (1 SoTT) transferred to Cosford from RAF Halton in 1993, absorbing 2 SoTT. The School currently offers Advanced Apprenticeship courses to RAF and international students in aeronautical engineering while the No.1 Radio School teaches electronics and communications disciplines.

RAF Cosford remains at the cutting edge of operational aerospace engineering training.

Boy entrants at RAF Cosford, 1954.

Test pieces are created by apprentices to demonstrate the skills they learn in training.

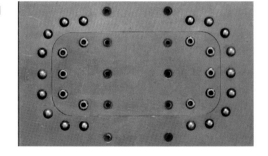

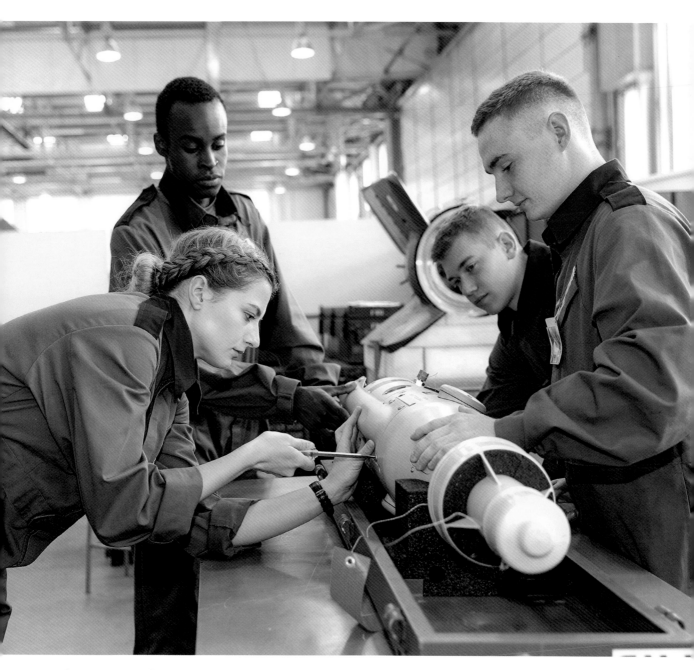

Apprentice Weapons Technicians at RAF Cosford, 2018.

RAF Museum Cosford

The RAF Museum opened in London on 15 November 1972 at the site of RAF Hendon. Aircraft not chosen for display were stored at other RAF stations, including Cosford. Stored aircraft at RAF Cosford were occasionally made available for viewing, and regular monthly opening of the developing Aerospace Museum began in the spring of 1974.

A civilian volunteer support group, the Aerospace Museum Society, was founded in 1977. The group raised funds, ran events, conserved and restored aircraft and shared its knowledge with visitors. Some of the original members of the Society still volunteer at the Museum today.

In 1979, the Trustees of the RAF Museum took over the management of the Aerospace Museum and two staff were appointed. The collection at Cosford continued to grow. Some aircraft were even flown in using the runway at the airbase, including the Bristol Britannia 312, Handley Page Hastings, Avro Vulcan and, most recently, the Lockheed Hercules C Mk 3P.

Aerial view of RAF Museum and RAF Cosford, 2010.

The team at the Aerospace Museum, 1993.

Under a new arrangement between the Ministry of Defence and the RAF Museum the ownership of the Aerospace Museum collection at Cosford passed to the RAF Museum in 1998. The Aerospace Museum became the RAF Museum Cosford.

Major developments on site have included a world class Visitor and Conference Centre built in 1998, an award-winning Conservation Centre (named after the then Marshal of the Royal Air Force Sir Michael Beetham) in 2002, and the visually stunning and innovative National Cold War Exhibition in 2007.

Future projects will build on these strong foundations to enhance visitor engagement with the amazing stories of the RAF past and present.

Volunteers from the Aerospace Museum Society in the Michael Beetham Conservation Centre.

‘ The long-standing relationship between the Station and the Museum is as strong as it has ever been with the two organisations working closely together to promote STEM to many thousands of young people. ’

Group Captain Tone Baker, Station Commander RAF Cosford

NIMROD R1
1974 - 2011

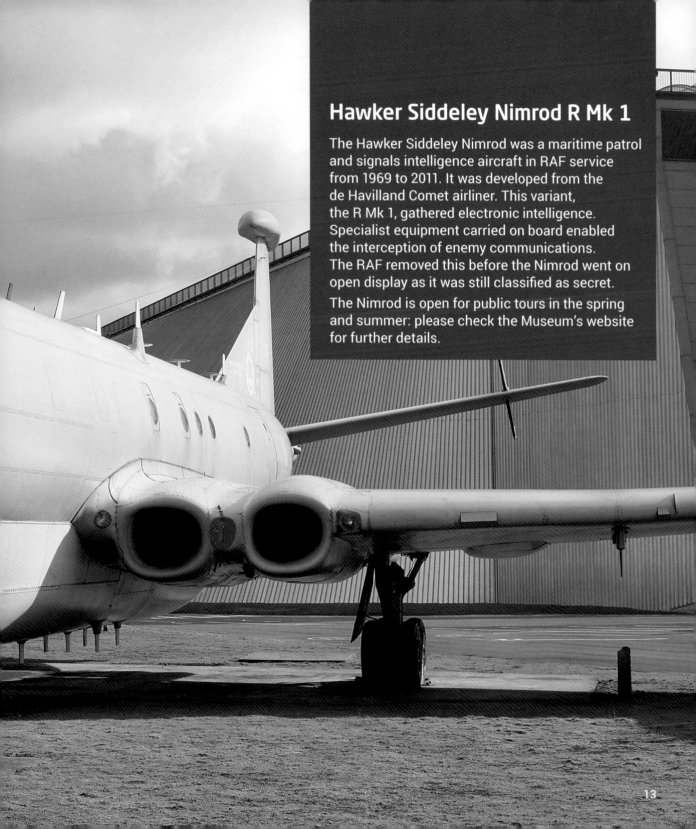

Hawker Siddeley Nimrod R Mk 1

The Hawker Siddeley Nimrod was a maritime patrol and signals intelligence aircraft in RAF service from 1969 to 2011. It was developed from the de Havilland Comet airliner. This variant, the R Mk 1, gathered electronic intelligence. Specialist equipment carried on board enabled the interception of enemy communications. The RAF removed this before the Nimrod went on open display as it was still classified as secret.

The Nimrod is open for public tours in the spring and summer: please check the Museum's website for further details.

Hangar 2
RAF Stories

The Royal Air Force's story is woven into the history of the United Kingdom, from its formation during the First World War to the vital role it performs today as the nation's first line of defence. In this introductory display, stories about extra-ordinary people and objects reveal how the Royal Air Force delivered its mission across its first 100 years.

The function of the Royal Air Force, the world's first independent Air Force, remains unchanged across a hundred years: its mission is to defend the UK, to attack if required, to support in times of humanitarian crisis and to move people and equipment quickly across the world.

Prepare

The RAF uses state-of-the-art technologies to deliver its mission, but its greatest assets are the highly skilled men and women who serve in its ranks. The service helps people from all backgrounds find the role most suited to their talents and trains them in world-class facilities, enabling anyone to go anywhere. RAF personnel are encouraged to develop their knowledge and skills to bring out the best in themselves and others, both while in service and when they return to civilian life.

Much of the high-tech training that takes place in the RAF today has its roots in the vision of Hugh Trenchard, 1st Viscount Trenchard (1873–1956) who has become known as 'The Father of the RAF'.

After joining the army in 1893, he rose to command the Royal Flying Corps in France during the First World War and became Chief of the Air Staff, for the first time, shortly before the formation of the RAF. Lord Trenchard later became convinced of the need for an independent air force and a core of personnel who could operate the RAF's increasingly complex technology. His belief in the importance of training resulted in three institutional training pillars: RAF College Cranwell, a Technical Training School at Halton and a Staff College at Andover.

RAF Cosford today is a centre of training focusing on aeronautical engineering.

> ❛ I have laid the foundations for a castle; if nobody builds anything bigger than a cottage on them, it will at least be a very good cottage. ❜
>
> Lord Trenchard

Previous page: The RAF Ensign.

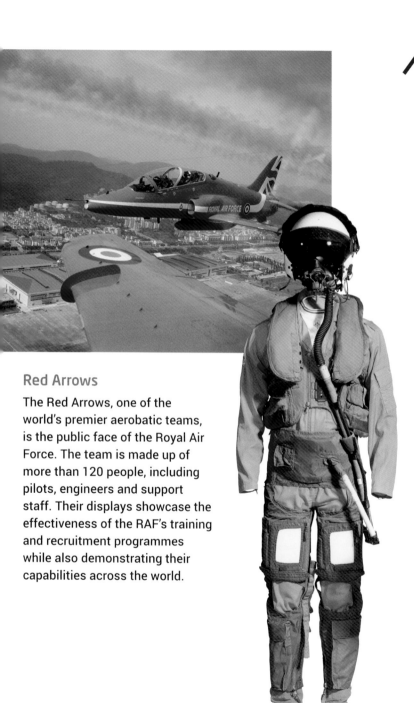

Warrant Officer Shobha Earl QVRM

Shobha Earl trained as an administrator and became the RAF's first Asian female Warrant Officer in 2001. After 25 years' Regular Service, she moved to the Royal Auxiliary Air Force where she was appointed Command Warrant Officer Reserves and organised prestigious ceremonial events. In 2018, she was recognised for her outstanding work on both No. 600 Squadron and as a reservist in general, being awarded the Queen's Volunteer Reserves Medal. Shobha has also escorted the Sovereign's Colour of the Royal Auxiliary Air Force on five occasions.

Red Arrows

The Red Arrows, one of the world's premier aerobatic teams, is the public face of the Royal Air Force. The team is made up of more than 120 people, including pilots, engineers and support staff. Their displays showcase the effectiveness of the RAF's training and recruitment programmes while also demonstrating their capabilities across the world.

Attack

Throughout its history the RAF has been an attacking force. Over many campaigns and operations, it has demonstrated the ability to take the fight to the heart of the enemy, despite sometimes suffering heavy losses. While the threat of attack can be a strong deterrent, when required during conflict, the RAF can deliver devastating force – from the area bombing raids of the Second World War to the precision delivery of modern guided weapons.

The seeker head of a laser-guided bomb allows it to home in on a target marked by either ground or air forces. In the 1970s the introduction of laser-guided bombs enhanced accuracy and changed the way the RAF conducted operations. First used during the Falklands Conflict, it was the 1991 Gulf War that highlighted the capabilities of precision-guided weapons such as the Paveway.

General Dynamics F-III armed with Paveway II laser-guided bomb, 1986.

Laser-seeking head for Raytheon Paveway II laser-guided bomb.

Fragment from the Möhne Dam

This piece of masonry is believed to be from the Möhne Dam, attacked and breached by No. 617 Squadron during the famous 'Dam Busters' raid of 16/17 May 1943. Of the 133 young men who set out on that Bomber Command mission, 53 died in the attack and three became prisoners-of-war.

Defend

Since 1918 the RAF has protected the interests of the UK from hostile threats in the air, at sea and on the ground. It defends the skies 24 hours a day, seven days a week. Its work, alongside the Royal Navy, the British Army and the UK's allies, continues to deliver vital global security.

A century ago, detection methods relied on direct observation and sound location, but by the Second World War, radar, which uses reflected radio waves, was successfully directing defending forces.

The wooden emergency exit door from the cockpit of Hawker Hurricane P2798. The cartoon cat figure, Figaro, was the pilot, Wing Commander Ian Gleed's personal marking. He led No. 87 Squadron on night defensive operations over western England.

Flight Sergeant Avis Joan Hearn MM

During the Battle of Britain, Acting Corporal Avis Hearn was a Women's Auxiliary Air Force (WAAF) radar operator at RAF Poling in West Sussex. On 18 August 1940 Poling was bombed by the German Air Force. Avis' building had all its windows and doors blown in and the walls were cracked and threatening to collapse. Despite this she remained to operate her radar receiver. Avis Hearn was later awarded the Military Medal for her courage and devotion to duty.

> ❝ The course of the enemy bombers is only too apparent to me because the bombs are almost dropping on my head. ❞
>
> Avis Hearn,
> August 1940

Support

Since its formation in 1918, the RAF has supported its people, the nation and those in need around the world. It delivers disaster relief and humanitarian aid. It ensures that people, supplies and equipment are transported quickly to wherever they are needed, whether for civil or military operations.

Repair and maintenance

Cutting-edge technology needs specialists to repair and maintain it. Today, major repair work is undertaken by industry partners, but RAF personnel carry out the daily servicing, maintenance and repair of equipment, sometimes with basic tools and under fire.

This is the standard RAF in-flight refuelling nozzle which has to be manoeuvred into a tanker aircraft's basket. In-flight refuelling greatly increases aircraft range and, consequently, Force effectiveness.

Senior Aircraftwoman Julie Brierley

Julie Brierley joined the RAF as an avionics mechanic in 1990 and undertook training at RAF Cosford.

She specialised in Jaguar and Tornado aircraft and served in Turkey and Saudi Arabia. She was the first female avionics mechanic on a front-line squadron and one of the first women to be based in Saudi Arabia on operational detachment.

Julie's post-RAF career includes leading the Access and Learning Programme at the RAF Museum Cosford.

> **Facilities for women on detachment could be basic and I remember at Incirlik in Turkey we slept in a tent separate to the rest of the Squadron and were escorted everywhere.**
>
> Senior Aircraftwoman, Julie Brierley

Saving lives

Operation BUSHEL was the codename given to the task of delivering food and supplies by RAF Hercules aircraft to support famine relief in Ethiopia during 1984–85. The RAF flew 2,152 missions and carried over 32,000 tonnes of provisions.

The RAF ensures that its own personnel are equipped with protective clothing, survival aids and other supplies.

In 1914 Princess Mary supported the creation of a fund to pay for a Christmas gift box to be sent to every serving member of the UK armed forces. Made of brass, its contents included smoking materials, chocolate and a photograph of the Princess.

Although the contents (pictured above right) no longer included smoking materials, this 2004 box, which contained

food, toiletries and novelty items, echoed the sentiments behind the 1914 version and helped to maintain morale for those deployed away from home at Christmas. These items come from boxes distributed to RAF personnel serving in Iraq.

Ground crews ensure the readiness of Hercules aircraft during the supply sorties of Operation BUSHEL.

Hangar 2
Test Flight

Innovation has always been important to the RAF, keeping the service up-to-date with cutting-edge technology. Key to this innovation is research and development. Prototype aircraft are built to test new designs and features.

Some prototypes enter full production. Others are cancelled, but not before valuable lessons are learned from extensive testing.

Flying differently

Some aircraft developments are attempts to refine and improve upon existing technologies. Others are the result of new and bold ways of thinking.

One of the major limitations of fixed-wing aircraft was the very long distances they needed to take off and land. This meant that they needed either very long runways, or very large aircraft carriers. These were both expensive to build and vulnerable to attack.

After the Second World War, the RAF started to look at ways of flying differently to meet these challenges. 'Jet flap' technology was an attempt to direct thrust downwards over an aircraft's extended flaps. This would improve low-speed flight characteristics and reduce

The Hunting 126

Built to demonstrate 'jet flap' technology, a series of 16 nozzles in the wing directed jet thrust downwards over the aircraft's flaps, which hugely increased the amount of available lift. The Hunting 126 had a take-off speed as low as 32 mph (51 km/h).

Previous page: The TSR 2 could have been the fastest all-British strike aircraft had it entered service. However, it was controversially cancelled in 1965 and only three prototypes were completed.

take-off and landing speeds and distances. Although adopted by some aircraft, jet flaps ultimately proved to be complicated and expensive to maintain.

Vectored thrust was a much more successful attempt to allow fixed-wing aircraft to not only fly more slowly, but also to facilitate full vertical take-off and landing.

For example, the Hawker Siddeley Kestrel could direct thrust rearwards and downwards through rotating exhaust nozzles, enabling it to take off straight upwards like a helicopter. The Kestrel (above) was developed into the Harrier, a very successful aircraft type that has seen service for over 50 years in the air forces of several nations.

 ... the Harrier ... went against everything you'd been taught about flying an aircraft.

Squadron Leader Andrew Edgell

Flying faster

Speed has always been an important aspect of an aircraft's performance. Whether it is flying fast enough to intercept enemy bombers, or being able to escape from unfriendly fighters, an aircraft's top speed will often give it the edge that it needs.

This, however, can present a number of challenges. Aircraft can become very unstable as they approach the speed of sound. Experiments were made with new types of wing to cope better with these high speeds. Some designs, such as the highly swept delta wing, proved very successful, and is still used on aircraft today such as the Eurofighter Typhoon.

Bristol 188

Flying at high speed can generate high temperatures, due to friction between the atmosphere and an aircraft's skin. The Bristol 188 was designed to fly very fast (Mach 3) to test for these effects. However, owing to its limited fuel capacity, the 188 was never able to exceed Mach 1.88.

Flying at high speed also generates stress on aircraft materials and components such as engines, all of which need to be carefully evaluated before full production can begin. The lessons learned enable future mistakes to be avoided.

The Fairey FD2 was an early delta wing prototype aircraft. It made history on 10 March 1956 when it broke the airspeed record, raising it to 1,132 mph (1,821 km/h). Not only was it the first aircraft to exceed 1,000 mph (1,609 km/h), it also smashed the previous airspeed record by a huge 310 mph (499 km/h).

Roland 'Bee' Beamont

Wing Commander 'Bee' Beamont was an acclaimed RAF fighter pilot during the Second World War who went on to be Chief Test Pilot for both English Electric and British Aircraft Corporation. Test Pilots had dangerous jobs which saw them evaluate brand new experimental aircraft.

When test flying his TSR 2, he had to undertake some hazardous operations. Once he experienced engine vibrations so severe it made him temporarily lose his vision. Another time he had to attempt to land with a faulty aircraft undercarriage.

Flying collaboratively

Up to the Second World War, there were many different companies designing and producing their own aircraft. Iconic names such as Supermarine, Hawker, Bristol, Avro, Gloster, Westland and de Havilland would individually respond to specifications issued by the Air Ministry for new aircraft types. From the designs produced independently by several companies, one or more prototypes would be ordered for evaluation.

This approach to research and development was hugely expensive. As defence spending shrunk after the Second World War, many of

Wing Commander Richard Patounas

Richard (Dicky) Patounas flew both Jaguars in operations over the Balkans and Typhoons over Libya, and regarded the Typhoon a huge improvement.

> And what a difference having massive amounts of awareness and capability ... it was a step change.

Wing Commander Richard Patounas

these aircraft-producing companies were amalgamated to save money. By the end of the 1960s, there were only a handful remaining.

Research and development costs also began to increase as aircraft became more complex and incorporated more advanced avionics and technology. From the 1960s, many aircraft were developed as international efforts between companies from several nations. The SEPECAT Jaguar (in RAF service 1974–2007) was developed by companies from the UK and France. Panavia (UK, Germany and Italy) produced the Tornado, in RAF service from 1979–2019.

The Experimental Aircraft Programme (pictured left) was designed in the 1980s as an advanced technology demonstrator for a proposed new fighter aircraft.

It was developed into the Eurofighter Typhoon by a consortium of British, German, Italian and Spanish companies. The Typhoon is the RAF's primary fighter aircraft and entered service in 2006.

The last all-British fighter aircraft in RAF service was the British Aircraft Corporation Lightning, which was retired in 1988.

RACE FOR
THE SKY

The rapid technological
development of war in the air
forced both sides to produce
better aircraft, engines,
armaments, equipment
and clothing.

Every country demanded aeroplanes
that were faster, or could fly further and
higher, or carry heavier weapons, than
the enemy's.

Practical progress was limited by the
availability of raw materials and a suitable
workforce for factories.

The constant evolution of aeroplanes,
equipment and tactics meant that
neither side dominated the air war for
long. Only in the later stages did the
Allies gain a firm advantage.

Hangar 3
War in
the Air

Powered fixed-wing aircraft had been flying for less than a decade before their potential for use in warfare was realised. The Royal Flying Corps (RFC) was established in 1912, before being merged into the independent Royal Air Force in 1918. For over a century, the RAF has been defending Britain's skies and projecting Britain's influence around the world.

First World War

The First World War saw huge developments in the application of air power. At the beginning of the conflict, aircraft were typically used for the observation of enemy positions, often relaying what they could see from the air to artillery units based on the ground.

Most aircraft were un-armed in the early stages of the war, but this soon changed as aircrew began to carry personal weapons such as pistols with them into the air. As the war progressed, aircraft were developed to fly faster with more powerful engines and were capable of impressive aerobatics. As they began to be fitted with forward-firing machine guns, the modern 'fighter' was born.

The First World War also saw the first large-scale experiments with strategic bombing of enemy cities. Although several thousand civilians were killed on both sides, the scale of the bombing was tiny compared to that seen in the Second World War.

Towards the end of the war, air power was seen as important enough for Lord Hugh Trenchard, Father of the Royal Air Force, to successfully argue for the establishment of an aerial warfare force separate to and independent from the Navy and the Army.

A popular and successful aircraft, the Sopwith Pup fighter first entered service in 1916.

Kevin Furniss

2nd Lt Kevin Furniss was educated at Wolverhampton Grammar School. While there he joined the Officer Training School and represented the school in rifle training at Bisley.

Kevin gained a commission with the Staffordshire Yeomanry in 1915 before transferring to the RFC in 1916.

He trained as a pilot and arrived in France in March 1917. Sadly he only survived four weeks before being shot down on 22 April. He died from his wounds a week later and is buried in Cambrai Military Cemetery, one of 400 RFC casualties in that month.

Previous page: Sopwith Pup (left) and Sopworth 1½ Strutter, two examples of First World War biplane combat aircraft.

Second World War Allied aircraft

Before the outbreak of the Second World War, most air forces had replaced their ageing biplanes with faster and more capable monoplanes. During the Battle of Britain in 1940, RAF Hurricanes and Spitfires were one of Britain's key lines of defence. The Spitfire's elegant lines have assured a lasting and iconic status in RAF history. However, the Hurricane was responsible for shooting down more enemy aircraft than all other air defences, air or ground, combined.

Flight Lieutenant Eric Stanley Lock DSO DFC

Eric Lock was born in Shrewsbury, Shropshire, in 1919. He joined the RAF in 1939 and trained as a pilot. He flew Spitfires and during the Battle of Britain in 1940 became the most successful RAF pilot, accounting for 21 enemy aircraft.

He survived numerous airborne battles despite being badly wounded in November 1940. He returned to duty in July 1941 but disappeared without trace during a patrol over Northern France on 3 August.

The Spitfire is the most iconic aircraft ever operated by the RAF. This example was operational in 1940, and is the oldest Spitfire Mk I surviving anywhere in the world.

> ' This officer has shown exceptional keenness and courage in his attacks against the enemy ... His magnificent fighting spirit and personal example have been in the highest traditions of the service. '

Wing Commander Eric James Brindley Nicolson VC DFC

As a pilot during the Battle of Britain in 1940, James Nicolson was awarded Fighter Command's only Victoria Cross. He shot down an enemy aircraft even though his Hawker Hurricane was on fire and despite his own severe wounds.

Prior to this he served with No. 72 Squadron and undertook several operational patrols in Spitfire Mk I K9942 displayed here at Cosford. He died in 1945 when his Liberator aircraft crashed into the Bay of Bengal.

> By continuing to engage the enemy after he had been wounded and his aircraft set on fire, he displayed exceptional gallantry and disregard for the safety of his own life.

Overshadowed by the more glamorous Spitfire, the Hurricane was the most numerous RAF fighter during the Battle of Britain. The Hurricane was tough as well as being easy to repair, making it a firm favourite with ground crew and pilots alike.

The powerful Rolls-Royce Merlin engine was fitted to a number of British aircraft, including the Spitfire, Hurricane, Lancaster and Mosquito.

Other aircraft types were less successful. The Boulton Paul Defiant carried all its guns in a turret behind the pilot. It was designed to approach enemy bombers from below, and fire upwards. It proved easy prey for German fighters, and was soon withdrawn from front-line duties.

Success in the air for the RAF was assured by hard work on the ground. Hundreds of thousands of engineers, technicians, controllers, drivers and other support staff – both men and women – helped to keep RAF aircraft flying.

While women did not take part in combat during the Second World War, many served as pilots in the Air Transport Auxiliary (ATA), including at RAF Cosford. Duties included ferrying new aircraft from factories to operational airfields. Female pilots were therefore able to fly the very latest RAF aircraft – even before front-line pilots!

Jackie Moggridge

Jackie Moggridge served as a pilot with the ATA during the Second World War. She flew over 1,500 sorties in a variety of aircraft including Supermarine Spitfires. A keen aviator before the war, Jackie attempted a parachute jump for fun. Too petite for equipment designed for men, Jackie's parachute failed to deploy properly and she broke her leg when she landed in a field of polo ponies.

Read more of Jackie's story at **rafstories.org**

The Boulton Paul Defiant was built in Wolverhampton, and this example was flown by a Polish squadron. Its unusual design made it vulnerable to Luftwaffe fighters. Defiants were soon relegated to night-time operations before being withdrawn altogether. This example carries the all-black scheme of a night-fighter.

Second World War Axis aircraft

Axis powers fielded a wide range of aircraft in the Second World War. Both Germany and Japan produced aircraft that easily matched those in service with the RAF and, in some cases, were vastly superior. The nimble Japanese Ki-43 fighter was able to outmanoeuvre RAF Hurricanes in the skies over south-east Asia, while the introduction of the Fw-190 in Luftwaffe service in 1941 came as a shock to pilots flying the latest RAF Spitfires.

The Axis powers were sometimes able to demonstrate a technological lead over the Allies in terms of new technologies.

Germany was the first power to introduce an operational jet combat aircraft (Me 262), although its introduction in 1944 came too late to change the outcome of the war. New rocket-propelled aircraft such as the Me 163 had very impressive capabilities, even if their combat performance was disappointing.

Occasionally, enemy aircraft would fall into Allied hands, either through capture or defection. These would then be assessed by Allied scientists, who would try to learn through studying the enemy's latest technology.

The Junkers Ju88 was one of the most versatile aircraft of the war, serving as both a fighter and bomber. The crew of this aircraft defected to Britain in 1943, two of whom, Heinrich Schmitt and Paul Rosenberger, were committed anti-Nazis. The third crew member tried to resist the defection and had to be held at gunpoint by Rosenberger while Schmitt flew the aircraft.

This was a night-fighter variant and was fitted with the latest German radar. This proved very useful to British scientists, who started investigating countermeasures.

Kawasaki Ki-100

The Ki-100 was a modern and very effective fighter aircraft that served with the Japanese Army. However, its introduction into service in March 1945 came too late to make a difference to the outcome of the war.

This example was captured in Saigon, now in Vietnam. After a few test flights and evaluations made by the Allies, it was shipped to the UK as a museum piece.

The Me 262 was the first jet aircraft to enter operational service. It was an able fighter that was significantly faster than any of the piston-engined aircraft flown by the Allies. However, Hitler's personal insistence that it be used as a bomber, a role to which it was less well suited, frustrated its full potential.

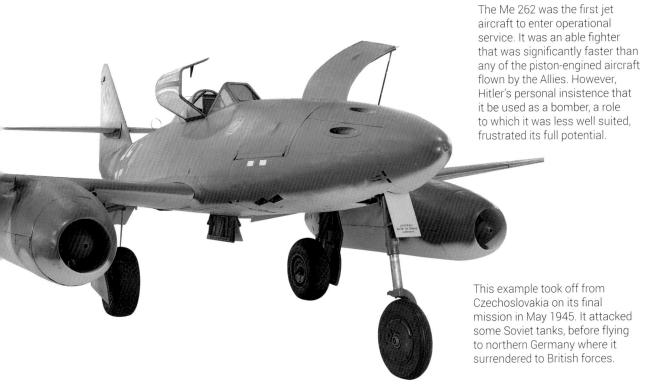

This example took off from Czechoslovakia on its final mission in May 1945. It attacked some Soviet tanks, before flying to northern Germany where it surrendered to British forces.

Post-war

Developed during the Second World War, the piston-engined Avro Lincoln (below) was based on the Lancaster, but entered service too late to see a combat role in that conflict. It served with the RAF until 1963, nearly 20 years after the RAF operated its first jet aircraft.

The Second World War came to an end in September 1945. Relations between the former wartime allies soon soured, and the period known as the Cold War began.

Technology which had been in its infancy during the Second World War was more fully developed during this period. Jet engines – rushed into service by the beleaguered Nazi regime – were further refined. War-time jet aircraft such as the Gloster Meteor were developed to attain speeds of just under 500 mph (804 km/h). By 1960, just 15 years later, the latest fighter aircraft were capable of speeds around 1,500 mph (2,414 km/h).

Piston-engine aircraft were not immediately replaced, however. The RAF was flying Spitfires well into the 1950s. The Avro Lincoln, developed during the war but introduced too late to see combat, was an updated version of the Lancaster. It was in RAF service until 1963.

Developed from the Hawker Siddeley Kestrel, the Harrier (above) was the world's first operational fixed-wing aircraft capable of vertical take-off and landing when it entered RAF service in 1969. This feature allowed the Harrier to operate from almost anywhere without the need for long runways.

During the Cold War, much of the Harrier fleet was stationed in West Germany, to deter invasion by the Soviet Union.

However, this example also served in the Falklands Conflict. It flew non-stop from the UK to Ascension Island in the South Atlantic, refuelling in-flight on the way. It was eventually deployed onto the aircraft carrier HMS Hermes, from which it flew many bombing raids and was damaged by enemy fire on several occasions.

> At the end of training I was sent out to RAF Wildenrath. [It was a] very, very exciting time because the Harrier jump jet had just been introduced into service.

Flight Lieutenant Suzanne Flynn

Superstitions and lucky charms

Flying always involves risk, especially in wartime. Even a well-trained crew flying a skilfully maintained aircraft can suffer an unexpected or unlucky incident. Aircrew often try to ward off bad luck and maintain morale by keeping lucky charms or mascots.

Charms can take many forms. Some are traditional good luck items such as a rabbit's foot, a black cat or medal of Saint Christopher (the patron saint of travellers). Others are everyday objects with a special meaning to the individual such as a coin given by a relative, or a girlfriend's silk stocking.

RAF personnel have also used artwork on aircraft to boost morale. Personal markings on British military aircraft first appeared during the First World War, disappearing between the wars due to official disapproval. By late 1939 nose art was becoming more and more flamboyant. During the 1991 Gulf War almost all RAF aircraft sported unofficial artwork.

Aircraft art

After the Victor XH672 (Hangar 4) ran off the runway at the US Air Force Base in Offutt, Nebraska, in February 1988, some new artwork appeared on the crew door. Many of the ground crew at the base were Irish-American, so the phrase 'I Ran Offut' when spoken with an Irish accent sounds like 'I ran off it'.

H4

Twinkletoes was the lucky black cat belonging to navigator Flight Lieutenant Arthur Brown during the historic first transatlantic flight of 14 June 1919. Twinkletoes made the journey in Arthur Brown's pocket.

Saint Christopher is the patron saint of travellers and a Saint Christopher medallion is a popular good luck charm. This one belonged to Jean Lennox Bird, who was the first woman to be awarded RAF pilot's wings in the Women's Royal Air Force Volunteer Reserve in 1952.

Lucky mascot Percy was tucked into his owner Flight Lieutenant Stan Chapman's flying jacket when they parachuted from their burning Halifax aircraft over Germany. They were captured and became prisoners until the end of the Second World War. Stan still believed that Percy had brought them luck as the crew all survived.

Wing Commander Roland Rat was a squadron mascot for No. 16 Squadron based at RAF Coltishall, Norfolk. He retired in 2005.

Hangar 4
Cold War

The National Cold War Exhibition includes dramatic displays of aircraft surrounding storytelling 'hot spots' which explore the consequences of the unravelling of the uneasy alliance of Britain and the United States with the Soviet Union at the end of the Second World War.

The relationship between the Western Allies and the Soviet Bloc was often very tense with a constant threat of nuclear war – but there was no direct military confrontation.

This period, known as the Cold War, lasted until the break-up of the Soviet Union in 1991.

Ideology

Underpinning the tensions between the Western Allies and the Soviet Bloc were two opposing sets of political ideologies. The Soviet Union was led by its Communist Party, which tightly controlled the social and economic activities of its citizens. The economies of Western nations operated along capitalist lines. While many Western nations struggled to manage their break away from their colonial past, most were liberal democracies that gave their citizens increasing amounts of personal freedom.

Both sides in the Cold War used propaganda to influence their citizens. Soviet poster art from the Cold War is widely regarded as being particularly striking.

The Cold War saw many advances in aviation, but had it turned 'hot' much of the fighting would have been done on the ground. The Alvis FV101 Scorpion was a light tank in service with the RAF Regiment, who used it to protect airfields and other military installations.

**Previous page:
Avro Vulcan and
Hawker Hunter in the
National Cold War Exhibition.**

Western societies had access to a wide variety of consumer goods. While the Soviet Bloc tried to present itself as a land of plenty, the products available to consumers were often of very poor quality. The Trabant earned the nickname of 'cardboard racer' reflecting the large proportion of powdered resin and cotton used in its manufacture.

The West sought to strengthen its position by forming NATO (North Atlantic Treaty Organisation), a collective defensive organisation that tightly bound most countries in North America and Western Europe. The Soviet Union countered this move by forming a similar organisation with its Eastern European satellite states, known as the Warsaw Pact. Both sides tried to establish or influence regimes in other parts of the world such as Latin America, Africa and south-east Asia.

The Cold War saw many advances in science and technology, particularly in the areas of aviation and space exploration. While standards of living increased hugely in the West, economic development was much slower in the East.

The Berlin Wall

Berlin was divided into Western and Soviet zones after the Second World War. The Berlin Wall, built in 1961, was designed to stop the citizens of East Berlin from fleeing to the West. It became emblematic of the controls on personal freedom that East Germany and other Communist states imposed.

Nuclear strike

The Victor entered service in 1958. After being retired as a bomber, the Victor was converted for use as a tanker, and it served with the RAF in this role until 1993.

Nuclear weapons were first used at the end of Second World War. Their unprecedented destructiveness introduced a new era of warfare. The concept of Mutually Assured Destruction (MAD) meant that nuclear armed nations could easily destroy one another. The threat of nuclear annihilation was one of the factors that prevented the Cold War from breaking out into an outright 'hot war' between East and West.

Initially, the RAF had responsibility for operating Britain's nuclear weapons. The American-built Douglas Thor was a land-based ballistic missile, introduced into RAF service in 1959. Perceived as being vulnerable to enemy attack, the Thor was overshadowed by the development of the 'V-Force'. The V-Force, or Bomber Command Main Force, was made up of three types of strategic nuclear bomber – the Vickers Valiant, the Handley Page Victor and the Avro Vulcan. These were designed to fly high enough for the RAF to evade Soviet air defences. Both bomber and missile launch crews were kept on high alert, ready to launch within minutes of receiving orders.

However, the development of Soviet surface-to-air missiles made the V-Force vulnerable to attack.

The Vulcan entered service in 1956. Its strong and distinctive delta wing allowed it to adapt well to low-level operations. RAF Vulcans took part in conventional bombing raids as part of the Falklands Conflict in 1982.

Ken Hubbard

Kenneth Hubbard was the captain of Vickers Valiant XD818 when it completed the first live drop of a British thermonuclear bomb. He recalled the subsequent mushroom cloud as ' ... a sight of such majesty and grotesque beauty that it defies adequate description'.

The series of drops was codenamed Operation GRAPPLE and began on 15 May 1957 over Malden Island in the South Pacific Ocean.

The Valiant was the first aircraft to join the V-Force in 1955. When its role was switched from high-altitude to low-altitude strikes, stress-induced metal fatigue began to affect its airframe, and it was withdrawn from service in 1965.

> The hooter would go ... and you would run, nothing else, throw on some clothes and run.

Peter Vangucci,
Thor Launch Control Officer

In the early 1960s, the V-Force's role was switched to that of a low-level strike aircraft, flying underneath enemy radar. Only the Vulcan, with its distinctive delta wing, proved suited to this change. The Valiant was withdrawn from service and the remaining Victors were converted into tanker aircraft.

The V-Force was replaced as Britain's nuclear deterrent in 1970 by the Polaris missile system, operated from submarines of the Royal Navy.

The Douglas Thor was an American-built Intermediate Range Ballistic Missile in RAF service between 1959 and 1963.

Defence

While the UK fielded the V-Force, the Soviet Union had its own fleet of strategic bombers. In the event of war, these bombers would have tried to drop nuclear weapons on British cities. One of the key responsibilities of the RAF during the Cold War was to stop these bombers from getting through its aerial defences.

The RAF had a number of options to stop the threat posed from Soviet bombers, including surface-to-air missiles and very fast interceptor aircraft such as the English Electric Lightning. As the Soviets developed their own ballistic missiles there was little that could be done to stop a nuclear attack.

If a nuclear attack occurred, the Royal Observer Corps (ROC) was tasked with relaying information about conditions on the ground back to central command to help them co-ordinate recovery efforts. Observers would operate from a network of over 1,500 underground monitoring posts, spread across the UK. The ROC was made up of mainly civilian volunteers, and was open to both men and women. The ROC was disbanded in 1996.

Radiac Survey Meter No. 2

Radiac meters would enable members of the ROC to assess the amount of radioactive fallout following a nuclear strike on the UK, as well as give warning of the most contaminated areas.

Civil Defence Corps armbands

Like the ROC, the Civil Defence Corps was founded to deal with national emergencies and formed mainly from civilian volunteers.

ROC gas mask

Gas masks would have afforded personnel some protection against the effects of a nuclear, biological or chemical attack.

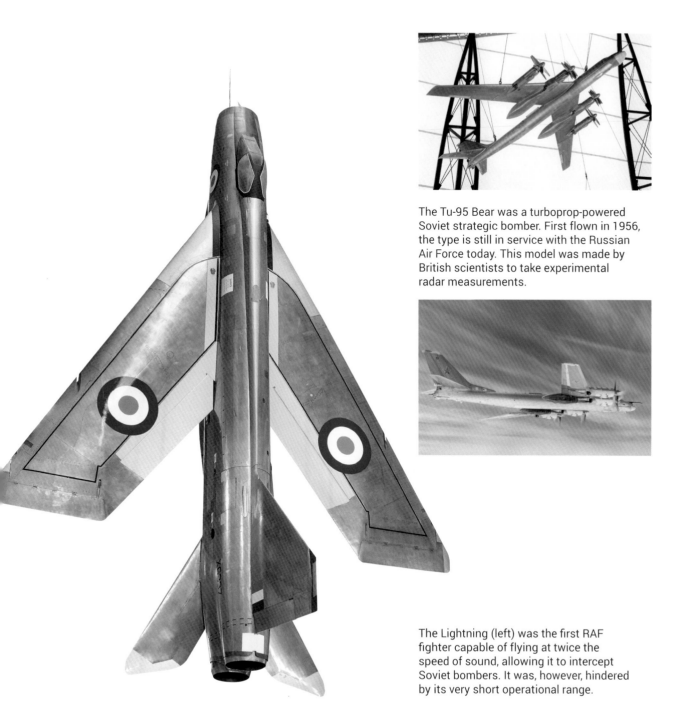

The Tu-95 Bear was a turboprop-powered Soviet strategic bomber. First flown in 1956, the type is still in service with the Russian Air Force today. This model was made by British scientists to take experimental radar measurements.

The Lightning (left) was the first RAF fighter capable of flying at twice the speed of sound, allowing it to intercept Soviet bombers. It was, however, hindered by its very short operational range.

Flashpoints

The threat of Mutually Assured Destruction may have prevented direct military confrontation between the Western Allies and the Soviet Union, but there were times when war seemed imminent.

One of the first of many crises was the Soviet blockade of West Berlin. During the Berlin Airlift, Western Allies had to fly in all the food and fuel required by the city's population (well over a million people) for a period of nearly a year between June 1948 and May 1949.

The Avro York was one of the RAF transport aircraft that took part in the Berlin Airlift, flying 58,124 of the 131,800 British sorties.

MiG-15bis

A Soviet fighter introduced in the late 1940s and widely exported, the MiG-15 caught the Western Allies off guard when they first encountered it during the Korean War. It proved vastly superior to aircraft such as the Lockheed P-80 Shooting Star and the Gloster Meteor.

Another crisis was caused by the Soviet decision to deploy nuclear missiles in Cuba, just 90 miles (145 km) away from the United States. The resulting diplomatic emergency is often described as the closest humanity has come to nuclear war.

The Cold War also saw widespread breakouts of proxy wars. Two such examples were the Korean War (1950–53) and the Vietnam War (1955–75). In both cases, the Soviet Union supported communist regimes which were at war with Western Allies. The Soviets provided material and financial support, and occasionally specialist personnel such as pilots, but stayed out of most of the fighting.

Tensions between East and West fluctuated throughout the Cold War, and there were times when the relationship between both blocs was said to have thawed. Starting in the late 1980s, a wave of social unrest within the Eastern bloc weakened the position of the Soviet Union, which was itself dissolved in 1991, bringing an end to the Cold War.

The American-designed Sabre was the first aircraft that could successfully take on the Russian-built Mig 15 in the skies over Korea. The RAF operated 430 Canadian-built Sabres for a brief period in the 1950s.

Protest

The Cold War was marked by populist anti-war protest movements. Issues such as the development and deployment of nuclear weapons and US involvement in Vietnam attracted widespread peaceful opposition, including the Women's Peace Camp at RAF Greenham Common.

XR525

G

Hangar 1
Transport
and training

All air forces rely on transport aircraft for moving troops and equipment. There is also a major requirement to retain a fleet of training aircraft to teach aircrews the wide variety of skills they must master before they can become operational. The Museum's collection of transport and training aircraft includes some of the largest and smallest machines flown by the Royal Air Force.

Training

Much of the training that takes place in the RAF today still takes inspiration from the vision of Lord Trenchard.

Prospective pilots need to learn a lot of theory around flying, but there is no substitute for practical experience in the air. Training aircraft are often very basic, but enable pupils to grasp the elementary aspects of flight before they go on to take control of more advanced aircraft.

Beyond the need to train pilots, Lord Trenchard also recognised the necessity of training mechanics in trades required to operate an increasingly technical service. A challenging technical course was established where boys as young as 16 joined up to begin an apprenticeship. Trainees spent three years at RAF Halton, learning how aircraft were built and to repair and maintain them. Graduates of the course were recognised as very highly skilled technicians, able to put their expertise to good use as much in civilian life as in the RAF. Sir Frank Whittle, inventor of the jet engine, started as an apprentice.

The de Havilland Tiger Moth was a very successful training aircraft, with 4,668 machines serving with the RAF from the 1930s until the 1950s. Most pilots in the Second World War received their initial training in Tiger Moths.

Previous page: The Westland Wessex entered service in 1962. It was intended for transport, ambulance and general-purpose duties such as carrying troops and ground assault weapons.

Air Commodore Sir Frank Whittle OM, KBE, CB, FRS, FRAes

Sir Frank Whittle is famous for his pioneering development of the jet engine. He joined the RAF as an apprentice at RAF Halton. He later earned a place on RAF Cranwell's prestigious officer and flying training course.

He went on to develop his theory of jet propulsion. Although interest from the Air Ministry in the early concept jet was lukewarm, Whittle persevered and the first aircraft to use his engine, the Gloster E28/39, eventually flew in 1941.

The de Havilland Chipmunk succeeded the Tiger Moth as the RAF's elementary training aircraft, serving from the 1950s until the 1990s.

HRH The Duke of Edinburgh made his first solo flight in this example in 1952. He has always claimed that the Chipmunk is one of his favourite aircraft.

Transport

Transport aircraft have always been essential for the RAF to support the deployment of British forces overseas. In addition to troop-carrying and supply-dropping, RAF aircraft also take part in medical evacuation and disaster relief and humanitarian operations.

This is a 1:24 scale model of a C-17 Globemaster 3, a long-range and heavy lift strategic transport aircraft. It can operate in support of combat, humanitarian and peace-keeping missions world-wide.

These large and robust aircraft are not designed to look elegant. However, the importance of transport aircraft to the RAF and to Britain's ability to project power and influence and to provide aid on a global scale cannot be underestimated.

Flight Lieutenant Julie Ann Gibson

In 1989, the RAF began recruiting female pilots for the first time in its history. RAF engineering officer Julie Gibson sent in her application on the very first day it became possible, and was subsequently the first female pilot to qualify in 1991.

She specialised in flying multi-engine aircraft and became a Captain on Lockheed Hercules aircraft, based at RAF Lyneham in Wiltshire. She delivered personnel and equipment to locations around the world.

> **If you have a dream or passion don't let anybody put you off it and don't let anybody say you can't do something because you are a girl.**
>
> Flight Lieutenant Julie Ann Gibson

Logistics

As well as supporting British forces on the ground, some RAF aircraft are often called on to support other RAF aircraft. For example, the limited range of fighter aircraft became particularly apparent with the development of jet fighters with their very high levels of fuel consumption.

One way round this problem is to refuel a fighter aircraft from a tanker aircraft while both aircraft are in flight. Experiments with air-to-air refuelling began in the 1920s, but the RAF's tankers first went operational in 1958.

These RAF tankers were converted from former bombers. Later tankers were converted from civilian airliners, such as the Lockheed Tristar and the Vickers VC10. These sometimes also retained a transport capacity.

A Vickers Valiant refuels a BAC Lightning in mid air.

Vickers VC10 C1 XR808 at RAF Kai Tak, Hong Kong, 1966.

Darren Priday

Darren Priday is now the Manager of the Michael Beetham Conservation Centre at the RAF Museum Cosford. Having previously served in the RAF, Darren began and ended his service career on VC10s.

> **I spent over 25% of my career on the VC10 – the Queen of the Sky – as we called them.**
>
> Darren Priday

Battlefield support

The RAF is often called in to support ground combat operations by the British Army and Royal Marines. Helicopters, with their ability to take off and land from roughly prepared zones, open fields or desert environments, are very useful means by which to reinforce, re-supply or evacuate injured troops in the midst of fighting.

During the campaign against Communist guerrillas in Malaya (1948–60) these helicopters were invaluable for carrying patrols into the jungle and their ability to evacuate casualties from small clearings proved a great morale booster.

Similar tactics would later be developed by the United States in the Vietnam War with their famous Bell UH1 'Huey' helicopters.

The Wessex became a familiar sight on anti-terrorist operations in Northern Ireland, and supported UN Peacekeeping forces in Cyprus. In its distinctive yellow livery, the Wessex also became recognised around the coasts of Britain as the RAF's principal search and rescue aircraft.

The RAF Museum's Wessex during a winching exercise while serving with No. 72 Squadron.

 Climbing two storeys to get into the cockpit is quite something else.

Squadron Leader Adam Robinson, who trained on the Wessex

In 1952 the Sycamore became the first British-designed helicopter to enter RAF service. It helped pioneer many of the helicopter techniques commonly used today in air-sea rescue and troop transport work.

Lockheed Hercules C Mk 3P

The Hercules entered RAF service in 1967 as a medium-range tactical transport aircraft. It could operate from short runways or roughly prepared strips, enabling it to deliver cargo and people close to the front lines in active war zones. The Hercules could also refuel in-flight, carry vehicles, drop paratroopers, and act as an ambulance. This Hercules was one of 30 modified to have a longer fuselage.

Vickers VC10 C1K

This VC10 long-range transport aircraft carries the serial number XR808 – leading to its affectionate nickname of 'Bob'. It arrived at the RAF Museum in Cosford in 2015 after a 70-mile (113 km) journey and was re-assembled over a period of four months. It has now been developed as a bespoke interactive learning space.

Michael Beetham Conservation Centre

The Michael Beetham Conservation Centre (MBCC) is world-renowned for the conservation and restoration of historic aircraft. It was named after Marshal of the Royal Air Force, Sir Michael Beetham, who opened the centre in May 2002, and it is housed in a purpose-built hangar.

Conservation

The team

Museum technicians and a team of over 50 dedicated volunteers work on a wide variety of RAF aircraft, using engineering and technical skills that were once widespread, but which are now disappearing.

The Museum also runs an award-winning technical apprentice scheme with six young people studying for their three-year Advanced Modern Apprenticeship qualifications at the MBCC.

The MBCC's technicians ensure that the apprentices have opportunities to build up a wide skills base. In addition to hands-on experience of general engineering, including welding and fabrication, the apprentices learn about skills specific to aircraft conservation – airframe engineering, carpentry and the conservation of historic fabric.

This unique environment ensures essential skills are passed on to the next generation, preparing them for work in engineering roles in both heritage and defence industry companies.

Past projects

Each conservation project comes with its own technical challenges – an aircraft from 1918 will need very different treatment to a 1950s marine craft.

RSL (Range Safety Launch) 1667

Built by Groves and Gutteridge in 1956, this vessel spent most of its service career policing and towing target ranges at sea in East Asia, at RAF Seletar and RAF Gan. When it was acquired by the RAF Museum in 1995, its metalwork was suffering from severe corrosion. The interior of the wheel house and the rudder mechanism have now been conserved. This long-term project involves the work of staff, apprentices and volunteers.

LVG CVI

This First World War reconnaissance biplane, constructed by Luftverkehrs-gesellschaft, was built in 1918 and was still flying until 2000. The metal and wood are in relatively good condition given its age, but its lozenge-pattern fabric has needed a lot of conservation and restoration work. The Irish linen fabric, with its intricate five-colour combinations, came from New Zealand. The project is due for completion in 2020.

The team is passionate about finding solutions to bring objects back to life, ready to be put on display for all our visitors to experience.

Some objects enter the RAF Museum's collection in poor condition, such as the Dornier Do-17. The aircraft was raised from Goodwin Sands in the English Channel in 2013 where it had crashed in 1940. Working closely with a team from Imperial College, London, MBCC technicians kept the airframe under a shower of mild citric acid for months in a hydration tunnel to neutralise impurities before painstaking cleaning work could commence.

Maintenance and transport

The MBCC team is also responsible for regular maintenance and movements of the larger Museum objects whether onsite, around the country or abroad. In 2018, the team supported the RAF100 national aircraft tour as it enthralled audiences across the UK.

Please visit the Museum's website to find out about opportunities to get behind-the-scenes access and see the work of the MBCC team for yourself.

Support us

The Royal Air Force Museum is a Registered Charity (No. 244708) and relies on the generous support of our many visitors, donors, charitable trusts and foundations, corporate sponsors and Grant-in-Aid from the UK Government through the Ministry of Defence.

Your support will help us ensure that we are able to inspire everyone with the RAF story – the people who shape it and its place in our lives.

Make a Donation:

You can support the Museum by making a one-off or regular donation via our website or by donating in person while visiting the Museum.

Become a Patron:

Join a Giving Circle and help us keep the RAF story alive for future generations. Become a vital part of the Museum's community of supporters – both national and international – to help secure the future of the Museum.

Corporate Membership:

We can tailor and deliver a package of events, invites and staff benefits to suit your needs and motivations, including client hospitality and venue hire in our unique settings. For more information visit: **rafmuseum.org/support-us/corporatesupport**

Fundraise for Us:

There are lots of ways you can get involved with fundraising for the Museum. You can sign up to one our fundraising events such as the Spitfire 10K run, take on your own fitness challenge or carry out your own fundraising. For more information visit **rafmuseum.org/support-us**

Adopt an Artefact:

Adopt a piece of the RAF story! Choose from one of over fifty objects from the Museum's collection, each with their own fascinating story. Items to adopt range from lucky mascots to aircraft. For more details on how to Adopt an Artefact and to browse the objects available visit **rafmuseum.org/support-us/adopt-an-artefact**

Leave a gift in your Will

After you have taken care of your loved ones, you may wish to consider leaving a gift to us in your Will. Your gift can reflect your particular interests and passions. To find out more please visit **rafmuseum.org/giftsinwills** or email **development@rafmuseum.org**

RAF Museum London

The Museum's free-to-enter sister site in Colindale, north-west London, also offers a great day out for all the family.

The story unfolds from the earliest days of flight through the four years of the first World War to the formation of the Royal Air Force in 1918.

Discover how the Royal Air Force has delivered its missions across its first 100 years, learn about its roles today, and debate its future contribution and technology through five fascinating exhibitions. Stories, objects, films and games reveal the service's extraordinary people, state-of-the art technologies, global alliances and partnerships.

Highlights include four aircraft that flew in the Battle of Britain, as well as iconic bombers such as the Avro Lancaster and Vulcan. You can take the opportunity to 'Sit in a Spitfire' or take to the skies in our flight simulators.

Our onsite cafés offer a full range of drinks, snacks and food. An extensive grassed landscape, reflecting the heritage of the site as The London Aerodrome and RAF Hendon, is perfect for picnicking.

Don't miss the themed outdoor play area for under-11s.

For more information and to plan your visit please visit: **rafmuseum.org.uk/ London** where you can also find out about our exciting programme of events.

Acknowledgements

This souvenir guide has been developed and written by a project team from the RAF Museum.

Project manager Jo Hall.

The team would like to thank all those who have shared their RAF stories.

New photography by Iain Duncan, RAF Museum Content Producer (Photography) and Peter Smith of Newbery Smith Photography Ltd.

All other archive images © Royal Air Force Museum or Crown Copyright, Ministry of Defence.

Plan by Robin Carter.

© 2020 Royal Air Force Museum.
Registered Charity No. 244708
rafmuseum.org.uk

Souvenir guide produced for the RAF Museum by Jigsaw Design & Publishing.

Printed in Great Britain by Swallowtail Print, Norwich.

20122/2

ISBN 978-0-9504788-8-3

Site map

H2 **Hangar 2**
RAF Stories
Test Flight

H3 **Hangar 3**
War in the Air

H4 **Hangar 4**
Cold War

H1 **Hangar 1**
Transport
and Training

P Parking

WC Toilets

Baby changing

S Shopping

Children's play area

Refreshments

Café

Simulators

4D 4D theatre

N